The Pursuit Of Consciousness

By
Omya Amayaa

MAPLE
PUBLISHERS

The Pursuit Of Consciousness

Author: Omya Amayaa

Copyright © 2025 Omya Amayaa

The right of Omya Amayaa to be identified as author of this work has been asserted by the author in accordance with section 77 and 78 of the Copyright, Designs and Patents Act 1988.

First Published in 2025

ISBN 978-1-83538-805-1 (Paperback)
978-1-83538-806-8 (E-Book)

Book cover design and Book layout by:
White Magic Studios
www.whitemagicstudios.co.uk

Published by:
Maple Publishers
Fairbourne Drive, Atterbury,
Milton Keynes,
MK10 9RG, UK
www.maplepublishers.com

A CIP catalogue record for this title is available from the British Library.

All rights reserved. No part of this book may be reproduced or translated in any form or by any means, electronic or mechanical, including photocopying, recording or by any information storage and retrieval system without written permission from the author.

This book is a memoir. It reflects the author's recollections of experiences over time. Some names and characteristics have been changed, some events have been compressed, and some dialogues have been recreated, and the Publisher hereby disclaims any responsibility for them.

"He who gives man spiritual knowledge is the greatest benefactor of mankind and as such we always find that those were the most powerful of men who helped man in his spiritual needs"

Swami Vivekananda

Many thanks

Mum, Dad and Radhe

ABOUT THE AUTHOR

Omya Amayaa is more than just a name; it reflects our inner journey.

Omya means 'born of the sacred syllable Om', carrying the timeless vibration of the universe's origin. The sound of creation and peace.

Amayaa means 'away from illusion', symbolizing the path of awakening and clarity beyond the veils that cloud the mind.

Together, Omya Amayaa expresses the essence of moving from the cosmic source towards freedom from illusion, a journey of truth, healing and remembrance that flows through every word in this book.

By writing under this name, I embrace my calling to share that journey with you, dear reader, as we walk together towards light and liberation.

The Pursuit of Consciousness
(You forget all the rules, do whatever you want; that comes with a price)

It all changed for good when I realised that I had not been awakened all my life even when I was doing perfectly every deed I was required to do, or I was expected to do. I am not saying that the side I am now on is greener because that is solely for an individual to decide. As they say life is what you make of it. But it felt like a long journey, a journey that I sometimes think I hurried through just to chase something which I am not yet sure of, and it's almost everybody's story out there - always chasing something, to be somewhere, to get to something, like a race, and it is all justified of course if you have to survive. So yes I cannot really suggest otherwise but my struggle with my journey was to give myself a right direction, a path, a way of life, something that we expect our young ones to get from religion or their parents, even sometimes from the environment they grow up in or they are expected to just imbibe the good qualities on their own , which most times is misunderstood or learnt as per one's own convenience. The credibility of everything depends on how it is perceived, with its importance or desirability being determined by the individual. As seekers, we rely on our environment to provide what we need for life.

And I continued my search, I was working each second searching for that one thing, an elixir to solve all the problems which I could perceive existing around me. And you see how everything is just a web. Everything when existing altogether starts making patterns or loops, cycles that each one of us go through in our lives knowingly unknowingly keeping us stagnant and the ones who be comfortable with that they be stable yes, but the ones who cannot help it and are trying to move, suffer. During my research, I found the concept of consciousness, which remains beyond scientific proof and visual observation. Various religions interpret it differently, but spirituality emphasizes its significance in human existence. It can change the game if its planted right in every soul.

I had no idea why suddenly I became the messiah of consciousness, I have no degree yes, but that is what it is about. the one thing that does not differentiate between a well-read person or an uneducated one, poor or rich. It is the existence and awareness of consciousness that exists within all of us, but for most of us unfortunately it never activates, or it comes to us so late that we have already wasted our lives without the presence of it and by the time it comes to us, we are already done with most parts of our lives. It seems unfair that humans, as the only beings on this planet capable of activating consciousness, should not naturally enjoy its existence in their lives. Yet, many people live their lives feeling lost and in darkness.

Understanding and creating awareness about the need of pursuing consciousness was a situation close to an experience when Newton explained gravity! He was worried because one cannot see gravity, one cannot touch it, but of course what fills the unknown and unexplained? ------God.

I do not know how it will change, how a wave of golden renaissance will arise and work for everyone in a way that they are at least able to start their journey right, but the word should be out. For whoever it resonates with, shall take the service.

So, the literal definition of consciousness is the quality or state of being aware, especially of something within oneself.

You see, the emphasis is on knowing ourselves, the need for looking inward, seeking our own truth, why we are the way we are. The whole explanation of wherever you are in your life tells you why you are where you are. But I must say what we see outside is mostly the opposite of it judging other people, blaming others for whatever happens in our life or to us. People who I feel are not in touch with their consciousness keep wasting their life on petty things that never serve them in the long run, because they are unable to step back and look at their lives from broader perspectives. And I am not saying everything becomes a cake walk when you are able to do that. No, life can still be tricky, but the only difference is that with you being aware of yourself, you never lose control over your life. You never reach a place of no return because your consciousness is always at play. It is working for you 24/7 to help you stay on your path. Every nerve in your body will tell you that you got to stop when you are taking a decision that would take not comply with your journey, so you would know, where you are going wrong.

I cannot guarantee if you will get to experience that feeling of being in touch with your consciousness in this lifetime or not, but I can take you through a journey which can at least give you taste of it.

Answer lies in darkness.
(Sorry, if you thought it would be easier)

"Whoever carries the light, must go into the darkness" Darkness scares us much. It used to scare me so much. Darkness is like that toxic love in your life which you can neither leave nor stay with. It scares us so much that we keep wishing for it to end. But one can choose to excel in making the most of one's lowest times. It is like never wait for anything; just become it from your side, no matter it is reflecting the same to you or not. But to understand the core of it, first we need to understand what darkness comprises of in human experience. As they say, where the devil himself cannot reach, he sends the feelings of Pride, Anger, Desire, Fear, Grief, Apathy, Guilt and Shame. And these feelings act as an armour to help the devil playout its final agenda of destruction. But is the destruction bad? Destruction is just as important as creation. What matters is where it happens and what is being destroyed. Is the destruction happening towards ripping someone or something off their life, love, health and wealth? If yes, then darkness is playing its role as an armour of evil. Darkness can affect individuals in various ways, either by making them its target or by causing them to expend all their energy resisting it. But it can be easily dealt with, with the realisation that you may let light win, by not letting the darkness have any significance.

If you can just focus more on making your light even stronger instead of using that precious energy to fight the darkness, you should do that, and this affects the darkness even more. Getting no importance whatsoever, getting no energy is the best revenge. Or if darkness works to eliminate the evils in human minds and environments, fostering a life that only human consciousness can achieve then destruction is good .The unpopular fact about darkness is that it is part of each one of us, good and bad doesn't exist for light and darkness to exist together, these two sides of a coin must exist for the balance to play out. But does that mean those who practice darkness more than light are demons? Or is it merely an imbalanced situation of life.? And I will say imbalance because even having too much light in someone will not survive in times like these where light and darkness exist in such a proximity. Society in 2025, according to Indian Vedas is called the Kaliyuga. The best way to deal with the existence of darkness, which is not only around you but to begin with, exists within you is to start out by working on your shadows. One is expected to start healing one's dark sides by recognising them at first You will not find these dark sides floating on the surface of your being, you will have to dig deep to start from the root, the times when you were not aware enough to manage your emotions right, when you were young, when you were dependent upon others around you for you to exist. Those were the times you suppressed feelings to be able to survive as per the demand of your caregivers, feelings like anger, frustration, standing up for your beliefs, not being understood or being a rebel. All these feelings when suppressed start to appear in most unexpected ways in your life that even you do not realise. Do not think they suddenly appeared, they were always there; it is just now when you are able to control your reality, and you aren't dependent on others that you start seeing them. You should be glad that you finally recognised them, because to solve a problem you first need to be able to recognise the problem and then work follows.

The interplay of your positive and negative forces can occur simultaneously. During periods of high productivity and mental capability, when output is maximized and a sense of fulfilment is felt, one might also experience moments of gloominess or disappointment as negative thoughts about potential future outcomes arise. These contrasting feelings coexist and can create significant internal conflict. It is important to understand that recognizing both the positive and negative aspects is essential. A person who can balance these two elements effectively may achieve success.

In Kaliyuga, something that operates just on the pretexts of goodness and light will not be surviving any longer than the ones preaching darkness. It does not matter how much one refuses to accept it; the powers of darkness are naturally stronger and more durable than the precious ones of light. It is only when light does not fade away in any situation whatsoever that they become weaker than light. Such a resilience used to exist in people in the times when people's lifestyle was not that challenging as it is now. For the generations coming after the 90's, you have the IT revolution and with that you have new platforms taking shape which can connect any individual from anywhere around the world with everyone just a click away. Now influence is cheap, and with that what is substantial and what is not has a thin line dividing it anymore. You may find this surprising, but being conscious can help navigate challenges posed by technology. For example, most of us know that we can always manage our social media with awareness, understanding how AI and algorithms work. Platforms like Instagram and Facebook show more content based on what you like, comment, share, and save. By making deliberate choices about your interests, you will see more relevant and informative posts. You can control your social media experience; it is all about being self-aware. Your surroundings will reflect your inner self. Clearly define what you need to shape your future self and seek it consciously. This will refine your feed algorithm to show only relevant content for your learning.

This was one example of how something like social media can be a game changer rather than being something which is said to have so many cons today. When you see newspapers and magazines talking about its effect on people's lives, making adults and children fall into depression by comparing their lives with those appearing to have more money, a bigger friend's circle, and millions of followers, when you see all of them making so much wealth off it and you couldn't, how useless it makes one feel!. Being conscious allows individuals to understand how societal tools can be utilized for personal benefit. Darkness in our lives is as important as light; we must recognize its value and not see it as the villain. Seeing it that way only makes us victims. A game nobody likes to play today because all it does is make you feel helpless, and nobody likes that. So how to handle the fire without getting burnt? Maybe by chasing the opposite? For instance, we all know the madness behind chasing the happiness in people's lives which is not very appropriate, although it helps/motivates one to move but expectation again is worthless. Because happiness is not a permanent situation but a state of mind, which may exist temporarily but cannot really exist all the time in one's life. Hence chasing the opposite of it or being able to make peace with the situation you find yourselves in, which is not happiness, may give so much relief because then it puts you in actual control. When you have no pressure to find yourself in the state of happiness all the time, imagine how much relief it may give you when you are not putting pressure on your mind to feel 'positive' constantly. Hence making peace with your negative side, thoughts and emotions and being able to coexist with all these feelings can give someone more comfort than suppressing it, fighting it and trying to get rid of it incessantly. Positive and negative perceptions depend on individual feelings, as what is positive for one person may be negative for another. Both aspects are equally part of us and products of our minds. Discrediting one over the other means rejecting a part of ourselves, which does not lead to peace.

To be able to understand its importance we need to know first what exactly darkness is,

Darkness is that force which exists where light does not exist. So, lack of light signifies darkness, but need of light also only arises because of darkness. So, light will have no importance if there were no darkness. You understand love only because hate exists, one understands good because bad exists, if there were nothing bad on the face of earth the importance of good would never be realised. So, darkness has all the right to exist It is the human choice, and choice of one's subconscious mind that must be able to understand the difference between the two and choose light over darkness in all scenarios and back it with darkness also if the force you are fighting is too dark as it is. As they say only iron can cut iron well; similarly, if light is powered with darkness to fight dark, you can imagine how strong it will become. Energy comprises of three important aspects – creation, nourishment and annihilation. Darkness forms that part of Energy which deals with annihilation, but here annihilation refers to the destruction of demonic energies. Nothing can beat it. It was a great shift in my life when I realised the importance of darkness. which I have in me too, like all of us. Nobody can be without darkness and denying its existence. As for me hating it was only making me hate a part of me that I have not made truce with. I was basically in denial of a part of me that consists of darkness, totally ignoring its existence on the pretext of being all about light and goodness. The blindsided view of darkness did no good to me because here was this part of me that I never fully sorted out or addressed even to myself and could never understand the power that existed in it. Hence, I was weak. Even when I was all good and sweet, I was weak. because I was in denial of a part of myself that I did not know how to harness in a right way and not be ignorant about it. Hinduism openly talks about how Shiva is the god of destruction. Destruction is as important as creation. By broadening your perspective, you will understand that darkness can only be overcome if acknowledged and guided. Ignoring the problem will not solve it.

Pre-fame souls

"Our work originates from the goal, not just towards it."

Today we see the world being divided into so many classes. We have all sorts of people out there – both rich and poor. We have several stories of how the poor became rich, or even of somebody who has generational wealth, how their ancestors had to work hard enough to provide generational wealth to their children., Everybody starts somewhere, it begins somewhere. Some people call these high achievers talented, genius and hardworking, some call them lucky, and some are called just blessed by God to have achieved so much in life. But have you ever noticed that all these 'lucky' people have a common denominator which in modern understanding is also called 'IT factor'.? Please ignore the blanket statement I am aware of the rule to speak for oneself and restraining from the generalisation but hypothetically, if we still use blanket statement for the sake of simplification, there is also the point of all of them being 'old souls', no matter what their age. All these self-made people you will find have a different aura way before they get any famous, rich or successful.

That common denominator also looked like they have a higher consciousness than the rest. When you see them, you identify this different 'know it all' aura about them which is irresistible to the masses. And that is why they can lead, influence and make a larger impact on the masses because they are self-confident people. You may not see them much in temples, but their spirituality level still has no competition. Some individuals exhibit a high level of maturity at a young age. This maturity can be attributed to the realization and unlocking of consciousness. While difficult to describe in words, this sense of awareness is perceptible to others. People who have not unlocked this awareness themselves may seek it in others. Consciousness is a key which automatically puts you on a path that takes you farther to unlock your best potential in life. You do not need anybody to push you to do it, it is a natural monitor in your body which promotes all the righteous ways of life without having to be told or taught. And that is just a start before you convert your deeds into right deeds and start creating a chain of karmas that do not come back to bite you. It basically protects you; it is your shield to keep your mind, soul and body in the right place. It puts you on a default mode to start working for your purpose. And this purpose does not have to be as big as going to Mars; in fact, the purpose cannot be judged by any individual. It is just what you are here for, on this earth, and how soon you realise it, and accept it as yours. You start the journey, and consciousness plays a big role in keeping you on that track without doubting yourself or judging anybody or yourself.

Living in a world which majorly focuses on money, fame, wealth and prosperity - not to speak of the root from which they all grow without even being asked- is a daunting task. In such circumstances, if you could manage the pursuit of building your inner self, striving for your overall growth and focusing on making yourself better, you will achieve more. It is more rewarding than, judging, fighting, belittling the wrongdoers and getting into the same rut as them. You conserve your precious energy which you could use towards building your purpose and not squander it on something that does no good to anyone because it is not your job to teach someone 'right' by stooping to their level. This could be best done by setting an example of truth by playing it out in your life. It is a difficult lesson that many learn only through challenging experiences. Some individuals must endure emotional highs and lows, witness dishonesty and manipulation, in attempting to address these issues directly. They try to reason with those who exhibit deceitful, narcissistic, and unempathetic behaviour. However, such individuals remain unaware of their actions until they recognize their own faults reflected in others. The harm they inflict on others is ultimately self-destructive. Individuals who endure any form of abuse can learn from their experiences and emerge stronger and more resilient. But the one who is inflicting that abuse stays far behind in the journey because at first, he/she must go through double the pain inflicted on others, fall over face first in deeper and darker place than he/she had ever imagined or he/she himself/herself had given to someone. Then when awareness hits and one realises how one never had the power (and no matter how many walls one builds to protect oneself,), one will have to face the consequence of every uncivilised act one ever did to the consciousness. This realisation is the purest form of the very idea of being human, and only then one's journey begins. If it is not achieved, they continuously find themselves in the same cycle again. One must take multiple births to be able to reach the same spot where higher consciousness is calling its people. The whole of humanity is taking birth and dying to be able to reach just there. The paths may differ, times may differ, but the finish line is just the same one which every living organism on this earth is chasing, and that is enlightenment by making the choice of conscious path.

People rarely start from the lowest dimension in life and reach the highest within the same lifetime. Those who are not accustomed to a higher-quality environment often fail to create one for themselves, even if they overcome challenges and work hard. They tend to self-sabotage. To rise to the next level, it is crucial to unlearn feelings of lack and learn to pamper oneself like a soul born blessed.

So, the Pre- fame souls are basically those survivors who were not defeated by the darkness. And they all must agree on one thing for sure, "that hate helps them grow quicker". These are individuals who do not lose their souls, as a state of soul loss occurs from traumas one may face in one's life. Trauma here refers to anything that literally has exceeded the capacity of the nervous system to process it. Humans have the potential to influence energies. If they do not harness this ability, their lives may appear to be influenced by unmanaged energies. Something that precedes the state of trauma in one's life, as trauma hits when one is unable to stay in their present moment and is pulled back into past experiences which keep their traumas alive in the present. When one keeps navigating back there in one's head, one is basically experiencing that trauma repeatedly. Because one's soul can hear one's consciousness, it is not in direct relation with one's reality but attached to what is going on in one's subconscious mind. Hence one must be careful with what one has got in there. In other words what one is feeding one's soul shapes all these factors.

The one important thing needed to be understood here is that one who feels most is someone who has a lot in them as gifts from the Almighty. All these feelings which shape into gain or loss in someone is abundance of energy that is left uncontrolled and not channelised. And gifted people like the ones that possess a lot of goodness in them. They are spiritual givers and are empathetic personalities. Sometimes these groundbreaking qualities begin to act against them as after all, these individuals have limitations of being human though they have divine qualities. So just imagine how much their true souls can be exposed to exploitation by darker and hollow energies that can feed incessantly on them without giving them the space to replenish themselves.

To deal with such a situation, these individuals who carry the light for the society are required to understand the importance of distancing oneself from one's gifts. One must understand the importance of not letting the two merges. Though spiritual beings, they must live the human experience as other mortal do, because at the end of the day, the very importance of a human is being present in the physical form in the physical world. One may certainly possess extraterrestrial – not so human like – gifts which are very rare to find in the great Kaliyuga. You may possess gifts that you may use to love humankind, which basically implies that you are just chosen to be the humankind's servant. You still must remember that no matter how much of a giver your soul maybe, you are not God yourself. So, you must divide the two and value both- your soul, and your gifts separately. The way when we watch movie, we can feel the characters in the movie to a point we even end up crying when there is a sad story going on, but we do not become the characters ourselves. We very well understand the division between the two. Similarly, we need to understand that no matter what characters we play in our lives, and what profession we are in, or what role we are granted as a child of God to complete for humanity, we always need to understand the importance of separating our soul from all these characters we play. It can also be called as soul retrieval. Which emphasises on the importance of 'grounding', or 'returning to self', back to one's soul every time one may experience any heart shaking experience, just come back to oneself. So, soul retrieval is nothing but just the creation of wholeness by bringing soul back to your body, again no matter how many experiences you have. By exercising grounding you realise the importance of experiencing the wow moment. So, survival that these Pre-Fame souls possess is basically taking control of oneself all over again, with their beautiful gifts intact. Instead of losing focus during difficult times, one can begin by concentrating on and practicing the three Ss of personality enhancement: Slowdown, Silence, and Smile. This can serve as a starting point. Flash a light on the people with higher consciousness viewing their lives with the respect to the idea of success? What if, instead of following a conventional, step-by-step blueprint for success. Those perspective lists of "musts" and "should-have's", you find yourself naturally embodying the qualities and actions outlined in them, not by force or mimicry, but as an organic expression of your evolving consciousness? Imagine beginning from a place of inner alignment with your goal and not from the sense of lack or striving, but from a quite certainty of who you are becoming. In this approach, you do not climb the ladder of success from the bottom-up out of pressure or insecurity. Rather, you live in accordance with the person you are already becoming. As a result, the steps on that list seem to fall into place in reverse, not because you are trying to achieve them, but because they unfold naturally as extensions of your being. You then find your tribe, your like-minded community, not to validate your path, but to reflect it. This is the difference between living in reaction to external expectations versus moving in rhythm with the karmic intelligence of your soul's unfolding.

A common trait among these Pre-Fame individuals is high emotional intelligence. This encompasses not only recognizing others' emotions but also managing one's own. Without this skill, they might react impulsively or avoid situations unnecessarily, hindering their growth. These individuals focus on understanding and regulating their emotions to foster personal development. They can clearly identify those emotions which have the tendency to alter one's reality. On identification they can work on creating tolerance for those emotions before they go out of hand. They can work on interpreting those emotions, their triggers, and eventually manage to regulate them right away even while being exposed to those situations against their will, they control emotional dysregulation by channelling their energy from anger and frustration into constructive actions to address core issues.

One needs to understand here that you are not asked to get rid of your emotions altogether as they play a very important role. It just means that we are required to avoid stressful situations where our emotions can play against us. Also, it does not imply that you are not allowed to feel your grievances, one is, but one needs to develop awareness about when one should move forward.

One's non acceptance of reality also stems from feelings like depression and dysregulation because the ability to accept a certain situation is the kickstart to move forward in one's life.

Pre-fame souls understand the power of emotions. If understood correctly, emotions like anger and anxiety are a powerhouse, it is the energy that your body gives back to you to survive the feeling of a dangerous situation. But being part of an advanced society and being civilised humans, we are required to be able to regulate that energy in a way that it benefits us as humanity or if not, at least that energy should not be wasted on making it worse for you. It can also be ensured if one puts a check on one's automatic responses, in the moment. Hence let us focus on not creating another generation of "Little emotional gangsters". Instead let us build ones who understand the importance of making it a point of not crumbling under emotions/pressure".

Pre-fame individuals recognize the value of identifying errors and constructive criticism. They understand that once an issue is identified and addressed, it loses its impact. They learn from mistakes and move on without letting negativity affect them, knowing they may not be the king of the universe, but that one can always choose to be a king in one's own world.

After emotional quotient comes Spiritual quotient, a term not many people are fond of but deep inside it is what the true meaning of humanity is, to be able to reach spiritual quotient. Spiritual quotient is basically the intelligence that addresses and helps in solving problems of meaning and value in our lives and places our actions and our lives in a wider, richer and meaningful context. Its true meaning is being human, or humans having spiritual experience. It's like that medicine for the mind which can keep you free from fear and save you from getting into trouble or putting anybody else in trouble, something that creates good karma When we see it in people, we tend to call them awakened or enlightened. It is like a game changer. Something that sets Pre-fame souls apart from those who cannot fathom the very meaning of it and reason for its existence.

Another thing that all Pre-fame souls appear to have realised is how times of crisis can be the most useful times for completion of one's goals. And they know how to seize that opportunity instead of playing blame games and complaints or facing disappointments. They make themselves more productive to slowly build themselves up for their future selves. All Pre-Fame souls seem to realize that in terms of their spiritual evolution which is the kickstart for them to attain the highest levels of consciousness, the lower they go, the higher they can hit. Just the more the depth the greater the height. They know how to take fuel from anything that is given to them from life, and they use that fuel to sharpen themselves and prepare themselves more for their calling. They understand that rejection anywhere is redirection. Any rejection or failure does not devalue the importance of the product you are building as yourself; it just means that a particular situation is not for the product you are becoming.

Pre fame souls by default suffer from this summit fever, they cannot choose anything other than following their purpose. They cannot settle for anything less. They do not appear to be stable by other people's standards, the reason being that they do not choose to be stagnant, as the consciousness in them would not let them sit and not do anything about the purpose that they have been chosen for. So, it appears that for them their purpose is the only truth, and success whenever it chooses to come is the only option.

Therefore, they do not have to force themselves to forgo worldly pleasure to follow their ultimate truth, they are naturally on that path, and that is how they truly become unstoppable. Above all they are truthful to themselves and to their heart's desires. They do not choose comfort over struggles. And here, the struggle is that change, it is the audacity to accept it; it does not matter where they are in life. If something is not for them, they are not greedy to keep holding on to that, they would rather be courageous enough to leave it, be alone and in discomfort if they need to be and then follow their real path.

How was the box of blessings unlocked?
(Must be above it, to be over it)

Once you hit that dimension, everything becomes clear and the more things become clearer, the more you feel you are starting afresh. Each realisation that hits you makes you feel you are born anew. Which makes life more interesting, and before you experience that, transition reaches its bottom and launches back to start a new circle with the improvement you have acquired because of your karmas, and with each ascension your skills multiply like it happens in a video game, when with each round you just level up. But it all depends upon you how much you are willing to make the best of each transition through your karmas and your approach in life.

The things that mainly matter are your intentions and your approach towards being flexible in life. But the hack is that you keep yourself in movement and never be stuck. Just learn from the experience- good or bad- and must carry on, no matter which direction you look at, the true nature of human consciousness is to circle back to your meditation and your calling.

It is the law of nature that what belongs to you can never ever be taken away from you, and what must come to you can never be diverted. Often, it is a funny sight to watch somebody fighting the inevitable results of their karmas and trying to turn them as per their requirements. That is nothing but the wastage of one's energy, and one may end up sabotaging the result of that situation even more. So, when they say you cannot be God, you got to take that seriously and leave things that cannot be controlled by you untouched. Wise it would be to use that energy into making things fruitful, to change things that are for you to change. For instance, healing yourself.

Once you acquire this consciousness, you may begin to feel like a fish out of water amongst people you are sharing your life with now. A whole surge of disagreements, disappointments, unsettlements, heartbreaks may arise in this situation for the person one may find with oneself because transition from being asleep to being awake has its own results. This sometimes leaves the individual feeling bewildered, facing failures and frustrations in life because the life one is so attached to when asleep must be compromised. When consciousness awakens, it may naturally start to change everything that is not serving the individual on their journey ahead, but people are not able to take those losses and start thinking that their lives are being clouded with bad luck. Whereas what they are required to do is to use their consciousness to identify the spiritual ego that is building up in one's behaviour and passing judgment on people who are not in the same boat as they are. Instead of developing aversion towards people whom you may see as lacking, self-worth, healing, and motivation of a constant growth mindset which in turn embarks from consciousness and self-awareness, these people need to create healthy boundaries. Wherever they feel the energy is not serving them in their higher purpose, they must follow the path of isolation. One can create wonders if one is left alone. The vacuum you feel when you isolate yourself, may make you create a world full of content. That is the power of one's mindful isolation. Gift yourself that for a change instead of staying in the situations you tend to always be, hating and cribbing about every day. That can be the best gift you can give to yourself. But that isolation would only stay until you find your soul family. When you start producing the work of your soul, by following, to begin with your hobbies, turning them into your passion, and finally directing your soul on the path of your life's purpose, you can rest assured that you are on the right path. Hence you trust the people in your soul family, as you would find each other. You have just got to rub the bottle right for the genie to come out. As sad as it appears, but one must understand that the core of one's soul must stay aloof and untouched to stay focussed to uncover the potential within, which is often hidden and waiting to be discovered. This can sometimes manifest as anxieties or feelings of dissatisfaction with one's current situation, possibly indicating a need for change or direction toward a more suitable path. Without understanding the underlying reasons for this dissatisfaction, individuals may inadvertently harm their relationships and present life circumstances, attributing their sense of failure to external factors. If not addressed timely, these issues could have long-lasting impacts on an individual's well-being. But if realised it just feels like magic, a gift, waiting to be explored, and tired of being put on a pedestal.

You simply need to work daily, accept mistakes, improve, and move forward. Focus on achieving what is clear to you at any given moment. The rest of the darkness will be brightened in its own time. And do not forget to love your god, that is of utmost importance, because loving god is directly proportional to you loving yourself and marks the beginning of the journey in the true sense. And if you think loving oneself means treating oneself with all one's heart desires, it is in fact quite the opposite. Self-control is the key to living life to its fullest, not following everything your heart tries to convince you to acquire. Which means knowing what is right for you and what is not and not listening to your heart to make you do something that is nothing but slow suicide. Loving oneself in the true sense means being able to protect oneself from oneself. And learning constantly to be able to do that continuously. As they say, 'Often wash yourself of yourself'.

But that moment when your mind becomes naturally accustomed to receiving all these realisations, when your mind awakens -, you cannot force that precious point of life to happen. You just can't decide when it should come to you, instead let the time decide because it comes to all, but it only comes to a few at the right time, at a time when they still have some life left in them, some hope, some spark left in them to be able to use it creatively and share with the world. So never ever force it, but you can always seek it, always want it more. You can put your heart and soul in ways of it and keep making yourself better and better until it finally hits you. You cannot decide when it comes to you, but you cannot stop working towards it too as it is said, do not quit keep grinding, it is all about timing. You just must do everything you could do, and then you just keep going.

It is funny how the very definition of a true scholar has changed overtime. What is now left is just about clearing some examinations and submitting a few dissertations and finally grabbing that degree. Whereas if we seek answers in our Vedic scriptures, we see that real scholars and learned humans should first possess knowledge, kindness, sacrifice, Dharma, and true character. And above all that, true nature of consciousness is peace, eternal peace, being at peace. Peace, because if destruction comes to you in any form, whether emotional, mental or spiritual, you do not want to help that destruction more by reciprocating with the same energy. This is almost impossible for most people to understand. Even if they agree that they believe it, it is one of the hardest spiritual truths to practice, being at peace in times of turmoil. When these individuals try to take justice in their hand, forgetting the biggest idea that, only God could offer forgiveness, and the rest is vanity they also end up in the same situation. The struggle of responding to destruction with destruction and then receiving more destruction in return will, finally bring about the realisation that they cannot take justice in their own hands, and they must give in. Then they become 'numb' which also is a form of peace, the only difference is it is the peace they achieved at the cost of themselves. And at the cost of their patience and resilience. And only after they lose so much, they realise that the opposite of reaction is not reaction itself.

And this understanding is also rooted in the theory of energy and how it multiplies, as power lies in the creator, "I created you, and I can just as easily destroy you". When one understands the power behind this saying, one can easily understand the power behind one's decisions and actions.

'You can be safest and most useful in your purpose when you don't bother to touch it and don't allow it to touch you.' Here author is referring to 'everything that isn't serving you in the moment', but still persistently exists around you, because being human has its own limitations. You cannot design the world as per your preferences, and you cannot afford to lose it as well every time you are in an unfavourable situation. So, what can you do, is train your heart, mind and soul to not let it touch you in anyway whatsoever. Instead use the energy you would have wasted rebelling it, to build your defence increasingly so that you can secure yourself from unwanted energies in the long run. As they say, 'Win through your actions, never through your arguments'. But what we witness most of the time is fighting, we just keep fighting it. Earlier humankind had wars to fight in over different causes; now humans are fighting amongst themselves. Seems like that gene is still playing a big role and this time it is not working to protect humans but working to waste the very gifts humankind can develop because they are too busy catering to the energy of hostility. The idea is to crush the roots of our enemy not just in its physical form but also in spirit. Once the spirit is gone, it will automatically stop existing in physical reality, and here the enemy is not another soul but the bad energy they are driven by which is taking humanity away from consciousness and making it more animal like. To target such a low vibration, you must go deeper than winning an argument and aiming on achieving the last laugh in petty aimless fights.

Consciousness is that default button in humans which if tapped correctly, automatically makes you pursue only those things that are worth pursuing. You do not waste even a single minute of your life here and there unless it is necessary for your journey.

"One can't decide, can't foresee, as when you give it your voice and try to give it a picture you limit yourself to that manifestation." True self lets it be and does not decide how and when it should be. It lets itself shape, and it is only exposed to the fruits of times when one is least expecting it." Here author is referring to how aiming at cash, cars, jewels to start with in the name of manifestation is not what a conscious soul does. A conscious soul understands that one must focus on the abundance, the intention, the feeling and the self-belief behind the reality they wish to manifest. One focuses on the skill they are naturally talented in; one focuses on the purpose they realise they are made for, and puts all one's energy in that purpose, that is the right way of pursuing one's dreams or without having to sabotage it, in any form.

Today the very issue of people with each other is that they do not act with as much understanding as they should when they are less considerate towards each other's feelings, lacking humility and are being condescending, competitive and toxic. They keep showing all these feelings to each other knowingly unknowingly and then spread hate in different forms.

So basically, they self-sabotage the light they have by trying to spread it at the cost of other people's sense of self, as they do not learn the right way of delivery. They do not realise that one is supposed to lead one's life by not letting one's aura, core and soul being touched in anyway by other people's choices of leading their lives as they want. One needs to master one's energy game, such that nobody can temper with one's energy in any way no matter how they decide to deal with their own energies.

Summarising to the very idea of rational detachment. Remember?

And if you keep being affected by the way they are, if you find their level of consciousness being lower than yours and their vibrations or tuning not as high as yours, you have no right to judge them or feel that you are any better than they are. , One must discard this very spiritual ego which can destroy all the work you have ever done on yourself. "As the law of attraction suggests, something can only harm you if you believe it has the power to". You have no reason to take it personally or judge it if it does not affect you.

So, this is how one can unlock the box of blessings - by unlearning most things they think they should keep close to their hearts in every phase of their lives. Hence to go 360 degrees like that, seems to be the biggest change to take place in one's life. Because as of now we see most people being programmed to find flaws, repeatedly, in everything and everyone. We are not talking about constructive criticism here. Does one's criticism ensure it is going to construct anything for the one they are criticising in the name of tough love? Seldom. We are talking about criticising something just because it is out there for people to judge. Something that we see toxic parents doing to their children and passing it on to their kids as a generational curse.

Hence instead of trying to set an example of 'being good, doing right by them' in the name of tough love and in the name of their betterment, by trying to change them and belittling them in the name of making them any better, one tries to control them. You become so invested in your mission to 'make it right' that you forget the other person is also running from the same strong sense of their consciousness. Thus, by not changing the direction of the winds drastically, try to channelise them smoothly in the right direction instead of fighting them in the name of love is the key. Live and let live vibes.

Consciousness : The Real drug
(Revolutions are not radical anymore)

Here we will not be getting into the importance of sobriety, as it is cliché, but we know this fact that drugs are cheap thrills for those who cannot afford consciousness. In fact, being in touch with one's consciousness is even crazier than any drugs existing around us. Drugs only create a form of imbalance to imitate the experience one would have had if one were in touch with their consciousness. Drugs are worse because they secrete hormones in you, which only destroys your natural system of dopamine production in your brain. Just because one feels, one is far away from having the real conscious experience which opens the door of your mind more than one can imagine, one resorts to these drugs. The best part of this natural drug is that it is not illegal, not bad for your health, and you do not get to lick the back of any peddler to access it, not to mention it is free of cost. You just need to afford to be able to be in touch with your soul.

"There is no problem so complex, nor crisis so grave, that it cannot be satisfactorily resolved within 20 minutes," if not in real, then at least in your head. And here the author is not referring to being delusional in any way, although even if you try being delusion to protect your peace, that is not bad either. It is important to understand that dwelling on a situation for more than 20 minutes does not change the existing circumstances; it only strains your mental state. Maintaining consciousness at a high level requires being aware of one's peace and not letting it be disturbed by unfavourable situations. Also, happiness does not come from wishing to get rid of the problem or wishing for the problem to have never appeared in your life or crying about a problem repeatedly just because it exists, by ruminating about its existence in your head. Happiness basically comes from solving one's problems. So, if one is invested in solving it anyway, that is perfect. As Kidlin's law explains – 'A Problem written down is a problem halved.' But if one does not do that by doing all of the above, it is a mere misconception that the problem would disappear by mourning about the problems.

So, if one is invested in solving it anyway, that is perfect. But if you choose not to do anything that involves rumination, then it means giving yourself more importance than the problem itself and letting your vanity get the better of you. It also sounds like making the problem look like a mountain by putting it ahead of your mental peace, whereas if you zoom the lens on the surface, you will find that the concerns become pettier. You may cry once or twice for the losses you face but there is nothing wrong in getting in touch with your emotions, but changing the course of your true nature or affecting it due to outside factors playing a vital role is the cruellest thing to do to oneself. Emotions can sometimes interfere with achieving one's goals. A person who is aware of their consciousness understands that regret is unproductive. Believing that the path not taken would have been better can be counterproductive. Instead, it is important to feel confident about the choices made and focus on making those decisions work, rather than obsessing over whether you made the right decisions. So, you are basically expected to keep pushing even when it hurts, the way we do in a gym, we do not stop working out when heavy lifting hurts our arms and legs. Likewise, regulation of the pain you experience due to your emotions is also important to develop emotional resilience in your nature which creates the base for consciousness to make itself at home in your life. Tapping into your highest consciousness is realising that your body, mind and soul are bigger than anything that exists outside especially destruction in any form. Instead of seeking love, care, and support externally, give these to yourself with respect, humility, and grounding. But as we know it is easier said than done, so whenever you find yourself in such a situation what you can do to kickstart self-work this deep, when clouded with emotions that become stronger and stronger with each unfavourable experience you witness in your life- you may ask these questions in all those situations, "What would my higher self-do?" "How would my desired self-act? "And you would certainly think on these lines, if you do not want to be counted amongst 'well- developed bodies, fairly developed minds and undeveloped hearts.'

Consciousness helps one to break free from being stuck in the cycle of how one grew up. The realisation itself creates a sense of responsibility in an individual for the way they are instead of blaming their roots and the environments they grew up in. The other meaning of blaming is saving oneself from taking accountability for where one is in their lives, and avoiding the self-work required to do all of it right.

"Knowing the fact, that a person who has the intrinsic capacity to absorb and implement my advice will only need my advice".

The people who are in touch with their consciousness understand that the problem does not lie with being uncomfortable in life, the problem is not being comfortable with being uncomfortable.

Conscious people avoid negative self-talk of any sort. They deeply understand the power of words and they use them wisely with themselves as well.

Inspired by the British Mantra "Keep calm and carryon". The very example of how having a healthy regulation of your emotions can serve you, can be seen in this culture. In the 19th century, books, poems, and plays often exaggerated stoicism and its principles. The National Union of Women's Suffrage Societies stated in 1914 that "the modern woman must drive back the tears; she has work to do." This idea cemented the 'stiff upper lip' mentality, which is now seen as outdated, but this stereotype of emotional restraint persists. Lacking control over emotions can disturb our peace. Thus, fostering self-awareness and emotional regulation benefits both individuals and communities. Also, the need to regulate one's sorrow, anger and fear even if they are not shown out in the society but in one's own heart has its significance, as it is said, 'one must not lament before it has happened'. Even when events with the potential to evoke low vibrational feelings occur, consciousness naturally awakens an understanding of the importance of promptly moving past losses.

To cope with low vibrational urges, avoid escaping into another toxic situation that only temporarily distracts from your original loss. Just to forget previous trauma one ends up into bigger trouble and that starts a new cycle of abuse. This approach creates patterns and perpetuates toxic cycles. Instead, one should bravely embrace feelings of sorrow, pain, and unhappiness, accepting them as part of life, much like happiness. Close your doors if needed and observe with an open heart where dealing with the pain takes you. I am sure the dark tunnel must end somewhere, but you must go through it. So, the best way to deal with unwanted feelings is not to suppress them or let them overpower you. One must avoid the two extremes, and deal with them just like one takes one's medication, exactly in the right quantity no more or less, to treat the condition. Hence deal with it and do not forget the reason for which you are doing this- to heal.

One must always keep this in mind, that whatever one allows to exist and possess, overcomes them at a point if not regulated right. Hence the need for balance should never be lost sight of...

As having a conscious mind fills you with a lot of energy all the time, when the person does not realise his purpose, he is unable to exhaust his energy. This energy then accumulates to come out as anxiety. Hence when you feel a rush of energy, which is bestowed upon you to utilise it for your purpose, if you don't use it, it just gets wasted or gets spent on things that aren't serving you, acting like a glitch in your life and in the lives of people around you. Therefore, whenever you feel that your energy is trying to come out in the form of anxiety, try channelising it in the right direction. And if you do not you will start feeling overwhelmed for no reason or use any reason as your trigger, which is a clear sign that you just need to start working on your purpose.

The very idea of consciousness lies in the understanding of how it is connected and is singular in nature. There is a oneness in all that one can feel, and as much as one feels different from another their consciousness is coming from the same source from where all the others, good or evil, have their consciousness. This concept was first explained in the ancient text of Advaita school of philosophy called *'Mandukya Upanishad',* which is also the shortest of all Upanishads, and it is in this scripture where the references of all the consciousness is given. And the source of it all is also explained in how everything is connected.

The Upanishad presents a vision of an interconnected universe with a single, unifying principle behind the apparent diversity in the cosmos, any articulation of which is called Brahman. The Upanishads teach that Brahman resides in the atman (soul), the unchanging core of the human individual. It is due to this law of oneness, that no matter in what direction you move, or which field you try to master, you always reach the centre of knowledge. As paths of knowledge are connected, everything that stems from the very source, its consciousness is also connected. Hence hating the other is like hating oneself in one way or another. Therefore, one should hate the game and not the player.

"Don't force what doesn't come naturally." This applies to tapping into your consciousness. It should happen when you are ready for it, not when you are unprepared for the energy. Because we do not want to forcefully achieve it and then lose ourselves in the process of maintaining it. And even if we manage to do that, it is more like an exploitation of the self. As Krishna said, 'Do not give wisdom to someone who isn't ready to receive it'. It is more like following the call of nature than to change the course of it for our convenience. In any case just know, you will get enough chances to show to yourself (just yourself, and that is enough) your true potential and achievements as per your capabilities, hence do not be in hurry to sell yourself. Just see yourself unfolding in your natural course and wait for the magic to happen on its own. The way earthworms are not given eyes by nature because if they were given, they might not be able to soak and survive the bright light and sharp ways of world the way other complex beings can. Similarly, if one is not equipped to handle the light of consciousness one would not be receiving it, but if one proves oneself to be deserving of it, nothing can stop them from achieving it. Consciousness spreads like happiness; if you are prepared to receive it, a single moment of realization can transform your understanding. From that point, your journey in life becomes significant, and you become the central figure in it.

"You are one-of-a-kind, and you can't hide it even if you want to". But the other side of this attribute is self-doubt: when you embrace your unique self, it can be easy to feel directionless. The only way out of self-doubt is through it: the more you practice dancing to the beat of your own drum, the more certain of yourself and of your path you will become. Consciousness lies in the concept of self-belief, on the idea of knowing one's path and wholeheartedly walking on it. And no path is better or worse, as 'sensibilities may differ' and not everybody has to validate your choice of path as that is irrelevant if you are standing tall in favour of your path. Once you reach that stage in your journey, with or without anybody's thumbs up, you will not have to stop, and you will not have any regrets. Wherever the path takes, you shall respect each path that comes your way with all your heart and soul and keep moving on.

You must be both indifferent and passionate about your journey. Indifferent to the outcome and rewards, and how others perceive your path. Instead, focus on staying true to your own commitment. Expectations or judgements about yourself and those around you is one of the don'ts. And that is how you need to see your work. You need to understand the necessity of keeping some distance between you and your work, you do not have to be bound to your work to show your loyalty towards it. Keep the work in its place. Unbound and indifferent. There is a thin line between 'good crazy' and 'bad crazy', and you need to understand that thoroughly. You need to be neutral, calm in all situations possible. You may feel that you are entitled to stand out and overpower the world because now your ways are different from most around you. In this case you will only end up squandering your energy and eventually exhausting yourself mentally and emotionally. We must avoid doing this at all costs because one's survival is more important than all of it.

You need to exist to keep working your magic, without you there is no magic. You do not want to be one of those who drops like flies; you want to be the one who goes on and on. As how long one can go on and on, depends upon one's endurance. One might stay invisible in those small moments, but that comes with the promise of sticking on for long. In the journey on one's path towards consciousness, God needs no faint hearts as his ambassadors. Concealing one's intentions even from oneself may help, in public dealing; if you conceal them from yourself, it may leave you unaffected by the failures and losses it may bring into your life. We must always remember, if there's life, then there is also the world. As the path to consciousness lies in following the intention of practicing righteousness, if one does not want to follow the above morally, it may become necessary to be adopted rationally. For instance, one way of ensuring the practice of righteousness is by following the path of truth. And not just to those around you but most importantly sticking to truth even when with yourself, as a 'lie' is the biggest hurdle in the process of manifesting. When you lie, you stray from manifesting your true reality. Words cast spells by shaping your 3D world when understood and acted upon. Lies, therefore, distort your reality and influence your actions negatively.

So just as the existence of anything depends on the knowledge of its existence, the awareness about consciousness depends upon the very knowledge about it. Whatever one can experience, is to be experienced with the awareness and knowledge that there is no experience without the above two. How does having consciousness and its awareness work? It is in the understanding that one's mind changes, but consciousness continues staying as it is, intact with you. Throughout. How then can pure consciousness be experienced? One can experience pure consciousness through manifestations. The realities that are designed through one's manifestation can help one taste the fruits of one's consciousness.

It is in this very understanding that your problems are not you; you and your problems are on two different strata. Hence you should not be defined by your problems. Consciousness helps one realise that nothing stays with you, and these arguments can find their base in one's fourth reality – consisting of one's pure consciousness, which is unchanging, and it cannot have any relationship with everything that is changing. Hence, you're reaching your conscious reality is your way to reach all the cosmic consciousness of those aware or not aware. Consciousness is a single thread running under all the tangible things that ever exist, and it is unchanging, untouched by all the realities that ever existed. It is pure consciousness without any objective or goal.

Hence when one masters the idea of consciousness one can master the entire thread involving it all. And one can easily make miracles come to life with it.

It is a process of following 'I' back to its source. Consciousness leads to cessation of the universe, it nullifies the very concept of everything because we see it with microscopic lenses, and we find out that 'I' is the totality of all. And with each 'I' we have a different universe or idea of universe existing through its lens. Therefore, there is that oneness in variety. And consciousness connects it all making itself a common denominator.

True consciousness possesses the ability to illuminate anything that it encounters, yet it remains unaffected by any of it. It stands out from the other and that is what makes it unique. What we witness as matter in the outside world is like the dream of consciousness. The way matter appears, it is the result of consciousness.

Recognising reality prevents errors. Enlightenment serves as a remedy that can alleviate much suffering in one's life. And consciousness plays a major role in that enlightenment.

"*You alone right now are real, you are real, what you inspire to do is real. That is the only reality, everything else is falsity*"– Adwaita Vedanta

Righteousness

"You must offer the patient your help, without becoming the patient yourself".

On the path of consciousness, it gets very tough to collectively agree on what is right and what is wrong. We are not looking to create another path for 'radicals' in the name of righteousness. No, we have already got enough of those. So, what should we take our driving force as? Many may not agree on what is right or what is wrong, but you can have a community build on what is good or what is true. So, when you want to start on your journey the right way and you know you alone cannot decide what is right, you may start from 'goodness'. Means you can choose to be good and kind to others while creating your reality. Thus, the best way to do anything is by beginning from a good place. Keeping that in your mind and soul, you do not have to work towards the goal, but you can choose to work from the goal. For instance, if your aim is to make the world a better place to be, then you start acting like someone who lives in a better world, all the ethics you imagine people possessing in that better world, you may reveal all those ethics in you and you start running from there. You set an example, a living example, of what that better world would look like with every breath you take. A similar thing applies to understanding the importance of being real which is another word for being truthful, and not taking the course of lies. Many people do not understand that the ones who lie or live a life of lie make lying the biggest hurdle in the process of manifesting their own dream life. When you lie you, by default set yourself on the path of not being able to manifest your reality the way you truly want, because the words you are using are themselves made of untruth and as we know words cast a spell. So, the words that are untrue are only creating spells in your life based on those lies which never last long. Not to mention, how your actions too are affected by your words which in turn ends up affecting one's reality. Hence when they say how a single soul can change the entire world, it is not even the aim. The aim is to set an example for all the others to witness the vision you have, the ones who want to get aboard are welcome, and others can continue secretly admiring that vision from afar, with due respect. When they talk about achieving one's goals, and aims, surely these goals may consist of materialistic accumulation that one may aim for in one's life and hustling to achieve them. Because when one is conscious enough to realise one's purpose, a number does not suffice, nor can one have a time limit. It is a vision, it becomes one's way of life, it runs in every vein hence the entire journey becomes the goal. The progress you make during that journey day by day that is the goal, breathing the air of your vision every moment of your life is the goal. But some of us mistake our learning period as our 'struggle period'. We tend to dislike and disrespect it because journey does not come with the shimmer and glory of materials and fame. We tend to find the maximum pain in the journey but when we get the result or we are at a point of time when we are finally considered 'successful' by the masses, only that feels rewarding. One should be most excited about the journey to be honest because it's during the journey when you expand your horizon of learning and experiences that eventually shapes your personality but because journeys are considered as an anti-climax, that appear to be slow in transition, sometimes almost unnoticeable , it is seen as a period that is strikingly less important and dramatic than expected.. The day when we realise the importance of the journey, each day when you are motivating yourself to move, to work hard with no promise of glory and fame, which is the real work. Respecting that period will define you when you have it all, and how long you can sustain it also depends upon that period and your approach towards it. Journeys like these appear painful because sometimes they come with making hard decisions, but these decisions that appear hard to take, bring the most life changing experiences in your life which decides the course of your future. The approach of loving one's journey would invoke resilience and determination in one's character, which would contribute to staying strong in the face of great hardships. The realisation of the importance of one's journey would also come from the fact that wherever you are in your journey now, somebody somewhere will want what you have. If we understand human consciousness, we see that each soul is at a point in their journey which may be ahead of others or behind, there is no winning or losing for anybody in this game. It's just the realisation that we all have our journeys, and the choice of its pace has nothing to do with where others are in their journey. Understanding this, you may find many who are just starting, and they may 'appear' to be far behind you, but that does not mean they will not reach where you are right now. It just means they are following you, hence understanding that wherever you are in your journey you are at the best space where you should be and being grateful about it rather than self-sabotaging yourself by comparing your journey with the ones around you. Just like the way you never seek to acquire the pain and hardships others face in their journey you should also not waste your energy in envying the fruits they possess by working hard for their goals. And if you face criticism for wherever you are in your journey you do not have to do anything about it at all. Believing in oneself is enough and indifference towards criticism is best, because if you struggle to make yourself believe it may seem like you are fighting the truth. You do not have to fight for something with such strong foundation as truth, it speaks for itself, maybe not immediately yes but eventually.

"One does not need to pluck fruit from a tree that is about to be chopped down. The fruits will fall by themselves".

It can be challenging to know when someone is genuinely contributing to a solution or merely continuing ineffective efforts. This difficulty arises because it is often hard to tell when an issue has been resolved. Additional actions may be unproductive if the matter is already settled, but individuals may continue investing time and effort, struggling with acceptance. Redirecting efforts towards more impactful areas could yield better results. Self-awareness and valuing one's time can prevent wasted energy. We cannot change the opinions of others as realization comes from within; external forces often seem like obstacles. However, self-improvement in response to observed wrongs can foster positive change. A flexible mindset that adapts to life's complexities is essential. Protecting oneself and ensuring personal safety and security should always be the goal.

In the Name of 'Love'?
(A message from heart to heart.)

The most controversial mind wrecking debate ever. Love and whatever that comes with it. Now question here is not what to choose, the question is in the attempt of the choice we make. How much risk are we willing to take and face the loss? It is not setting oneself up for failure – no. It is about saving oneself from the hurt one can be in as the result of its failure. And the strangest part about it all is that if we see, each one of us has a different definition of what love looks like. Sometimes that belief in it works for you sometimes it does not, and heartbreak is so common now, that they have started saying, 'everybody goes through heartbreak'. As if heartbreak is a birthright. As if we deserve it. We deserve to face the loss. The cause of concern is not when one chooses to try one's luck in love, but it is when one goes through breakup or divorce, it is a huge deal in the world even today. Accept it or not, the fear of failure has stopped so many from loving or believing in the institution they call marriage. It is a social crisis, yet nobody can do anything Heartbreak feels like that darkness, that pain yes, which may help one grow up drastically in life. But it takes a lot from one's soul because one must give their all to be in love, and if they choose not to, their life is not complete. As much as love sounds like a win-win situation, in today's world it has become a losing game. So, the conclusion is, a loved one must lose oneself because 'adjustment' is everything when one becomes two, but because there seems to be no clear boundaries as to how much adjustment one must make, one tends to lose their value, their individuality, the motivation to grow. Which spirals back to losing the very basis of that relationship. And that is when the two people long for 'novelty' and 'spark', which is now lost because the two people are just shadowing each other in the process of becoming one. You lose what you both separately had to pour in that relationship to make it a teamwork. If not addressed properly, one partner may experience insecurities, trust issues, and a lack of feeling loved and understood. Conversely, the other partner might eventually feel stagnant in the relationship without growth, possibly leading to extramarital affairs or seeking companionship elsewhere. This cycle can continue if both partners do not engage in self-reflection and healing before entering the relationship. Consequently, this pattern can result in repeated heartbreaks and loss of relationships.

The essence of love and relationships often gets overshadowed by the mentality of making sacrifices for one another. Over time, love becomes a cycle of mutual sacrifice, where increased dependence and needs arise from this dynamic. True love thrives between two independent individuals who stay together consciously and unconsciously, without overshadowing each other in the name of 'love'.

As great minds have said, in the case of relationships the hidden secret is the very understanding of this final truth, what is meant to be, will be, try it yourself, don't ever pay a thought to it, don't ever waste a single thought on what can be or ought to be with a person, as that's a total waste of your time and energy. That is why they say, "Matches are made in heaven, they are not made on earth" because you cannot make them happen, not at least the ideal ones you expect. It does not mean that you completely stop working on your relationships, which is not the intention. The intention is whatever you decide to do it should just feel right in your gut. Listen to your gut. And do not work on a relationship at the cost of yourself. That is not what an ideal relationship would demand from you; only the ones that are surviving off you not the ones working for you.

Relationships thrive when both people meet halfway on common ground. However, many remain trapped in the cycles of their upbringing, never reaching mutual understanding. This is exacerbated by insecurities, leading to repeated patterns where small issues become magnified and attract more negativity. We think we are learning, but with that we tend to imbibe those red flags and end up showing to the next person coming into our lives, creating the same old loops. It is just roles that keep reversing. One time you get hurt, next you hurt someone. It just looks like a ping pong game of hormones if you observe from a distance. Dopamine and oxytocin are hormones which make us feel good and want to repeat behaviours in search of the same feeling over and over again. They are released at elevated levels when we are in love, but when heartbreak, these hormone levels drop and are replaced with the stress hormone cortisol. Eventually we see people becoming thick skinned because it is always survival of the fittest. But why can't we just get it right, or if it gets wrong, why has it become a question of do or die in our society? It sounds anything but friendly, and all this explains why we have the concept of brahmacharya (people who never get married or get into a relationship) in Hinduism and nuns and priests in Christianity, and then we have Buddhism, most famous for following celibacy. Why set oneself up for trouble when it is only what today's institutions and society have been designed for? Probably that is why they tend to cover up with sayings like 'marriage is hard'.

But yes, if two people think or at least feel that they have found love, what the two should do afterwards, is just that both go together in praising God. That is the finish line, before you get into any vacuum of what is next? Just fill up that empty space with everything about God, but you both must be on same page for that, with the same level of devotion to aim wholeheartedly for salvation together.

Murphy's law to Yhprum's law

(The grass is rarely greener; it just has not been stepped on by your expectations yet)

One thing that people who are not so aware of themselves, do not understand is the very correlation of Yhprum's law with Murphy's law. We all know Murphy's law which says that anything that can go wrong will go wrong. But rarely do people know about Yhprum's law, which says anything that can go right, will go right. Now a mind must choose - and it is going to be subjective in nature - which side they want to be on.

How can this work for everyone? Identify your patterns and loops, then simply apply reverse psychology. If you constantly chase happiness, you might feel its absence more. Accepting neutrality instead can invite genuine happiness without feeling the lack. This approach offers relief by shifting focus away from always being positive and allowing peace to come naturally. It is often more beneficial to acknowledge and accept one's negative thoughts and emotions, rather than constantly attempting to suppress or eliminate them. Coexisting with these aspects of oneself can provide greater comfort and peace of mind.

At the end of the day, it is just based on one's perception- negative/positive. What may be beneficial for one person might not be for another. By examining both perspectives objectively, without the influence of feelings or emotions, it becomes clear that both sides are equally integral to our understanding and experience. And discrediting the one over the other is as if you are totally discriminating one part of yourself from the other.

The people who function under the idea of Murphy's law, tend to base everything their life could offer, on the verge of losing. And you see it in the form of fear amongst people, more in those people who are generally living in some lack, like lack of money, confidence and resources. For instance, we can witness this in the very common mentality that exists amongst such people that they must keep struggling or working hard to sustain or even deserve anything they desire. Not to forget the feelings of guilt and regret that is instilled in people about choosing to have 'fun' over 'work'. That is another framework imposed by these societies on their kids, who later grow up to be chained to these ideas and are never able to live their life freely. Emphasising upon hard work is not wrong, but how it is perceived nowadays is wrong; the idea is not to kill yourself in the process just to be able to reach a level of satisfaction that you deserve, that you are seeking. Instead the idea is to like something you do so much that you don't even realise it has become such a unique part of your life that it never leaves you, which looks like you working hard for it yes, but in reality it is all you know you want to work on, and don't want it any other way. The intention changes everything and following Yhphrum's law over Murphy's changes your entire viewpoint towards life resulting in efforts and actions that lead into directions which would work in so many better ways for you.

Believing in such a mentality of lack sets you up for zero sum game situation in life, a situation in which one person or group can win something only by causing another person or group to lose it. If only we could see the broader reality: that abundance is limitless and meant for all, and there is no need to snatch, compare, or wish less for others just to feel whole ourselves.

The journey from Murphy's to Yhphrum's involves a bottom-up approach. This method reverses the process of how tasks are conventionally approached. Instead of following instructions to achieve a goal, one starts with the intention of having already achieved it and plans actions based on that premise. This approach can significantly impact people's lives.

Some people live by the saying that your present actions decide your future, but what if we see it as your future guiding your present actions - imagine how your actions, your intentions and approach will change.

This concept can be further illustrated by the example of how when an individual undertakes a task with the primary intention of fulfilling personal desires and expectations, specifically for achieving happiness as an outcome, they are likely to encounter disappointment. The pursuit of happiness under these conditions often results in sadness. Moreover, individuals may unknowingly become addicted to this relentless chase, leading them to perpetually seek happiness throughout their lives. Even if circumstances permit happiness, such individuals may remain discontent due to starting their journey with a sense of its absence. This continual cycle results in persistent dissatisfaction, regardless of their achievements. Therefore, the mindset or principles (such as Murphy's Law or Yhprum's Law) on which one bases their efforts significantly influences whether their pursuits commence in positivity or negativity.

Hence the intention behind performing any act matters, as what deeply matters is for one to keep going not only when things are in favour but on the days when they do not seem to be in favour at all. And this intention decides how honest one is with oneself and one's purpose and how much one is committed. Maybe you move slower than the other days, but you are still moving unhindered and unaffected.

Tale of Illusion: Product of 5th dimension?

"Don't shoot the messenger".

To begin with, let us just explain what illusion refers to in layman's language. An illusion is a misrepresentation of a 'real' sensory stimulus- that is, an interpretation that contradicts objective 'reality' as defined by general agreement. For example, a child who perceives tree branches at night as if they are goblins may be said to be having an illusion.

An illusion can also refer to a sensory distortion that can fool a person's senses. Illusions can involve any of the senses, but visual (optical) illusions are the ones best understood by science. Illusion occurs when a situation distorts a person's capacity for depth and motion perception and perceptual constancy.

"Miracles are new findings, which already existed but were never known".

We already live in this world and are typically aware of how 3rd and 4th dimensions have played out for us. We understand time and space and how they exist with relation to other things. So, nothing seems to be the ultimate reality but is just a part of what we call 'truth' which exists in combination with everything else.

As per science we are not sure what the 5th dimension comprises of. Something we are sure of, is that the 5th dimension is a micro-dimension which we cannot pinpoint, but which is accepted in physics and mathematics. Science has backed the 5th dimension, though we know that it is difficult to directly observe it. We are already living in the 5th dimension but are not aware of it. Or maybe we are not aware of the long-lasting impact this 5th dimension is playing out, in our lives, the way illusion is. Today we are living in a world which lives and judges on face value. We make decisions and base our judgements on everything around us just by the images we see, and newspaper we read.

It is like how we find ourselves so much better in the changing room when we choose a dress, but the same dress when worn without all the factors that were affecting the plain sight of it in the changing room, looks so ordinary. It is a very minute example of what illusion looks like on a wider level.

Most things that we see around us is not reputation built on firsthand information but through everything that is projected through the platforms which acts as third party. In the IT revolutionised world we live in, we can see how most opinions are shaped just based on what we read, watch and listen through all the gadgets like TV, mobile phones, magazines, novels, social networking platforms or apps that we have become so dependent on.

These gadgets collectively create an illusionary world that we all become part of, knowingly or unknowingly. For example, seeing a friend posting happily with their spouse may lead one to assume they have a happy married life. Similarly, observing someone with a pleasant appearance, branded clothes, and numerous followers on TikTok may give the impression of a fortunate life. Living in the world of Kardashians, what do you think they mastered to be as influential as they are? They mastered illusion. The illusions promoted often ignore the real challenges individuals face. While something may benefit one person, it does not mean others will find value in it.

But this capacity to fathom is declining due to illusion now clouding everybody's insight.

This distorts individuals' judgment, leading them to base their lives on illusions that are only dispelled after significant moments of enlightenment, or a profound awareness is achieved.

In contemporary society, numerous elements are designed to enhance the influence of illusion. From makeup and high-end fashion to application of filters and music, from feigned smiles to pretensions of wealth, every aspect contributes to constructing a world steeped in illusion, creating a reality that is significantly detached from authenticity. Consequently, truth has become increasingly subjective.

To navigate this paradigm effectively, one must master the art of illusion without becoming subjugated by it, particularly if not leveraging it to manipulate others. In this context, truth is no longer anchored in one's personality, intellect, or actions within the second, third, or fourth dimensions. An optimal approach involves maintaining a stable fourth dimension, separate from the second and third, thereby enabling access to higher consciousness. The interplay of these dimensions culminates in the contemporary game of illusion, which manifests as the fifth dimension in today's world.

Yet it is a world completely independent of all, that is the paradox, and this hope lies in the game of illusion if one can play it right. The illusion game is so powerful that it has the capacity to mould people's emotions. So, all the emotions and how they play out is also the result of illusion. As what you can illustrate in your head is only seen on your face in the form of emotions.

When people function in 5th dimension, they are not out of touch with daily realities. In fact, they have mastered these realities so well that now they are using the same to play the reality itself and changing the narrative as they desire them to be, hence consciousness vibrating that high makes these people extremely alert and bright. They see things that are in demand in other people's deepest dreams and darkest desires, and playout those things. Since they draw from a vast storehouse of energy and a broad evolutionary vantage point, they even do unfamiliar tasks with confidence—as if they had performed it a thousand times. Nothing seems strange and awkward to them as they have tapped in that highest form of consciousness in which humankind is known to be existing. Everything for them seems familiar, and they naturally bring grace into every department of life.

"When my results are revealed, humanity will be like an ant heap stirred up with a stick."- Tesla.

The reference to we living a life of illusion has also been backed by many great scientists and authors. According to theoretical physicist Carlo Rovelli, time is an illusion: our naïve perception of its flow does not correspond to physical reality. Indeed, as Rovelli argues in The Order of Time, much more is illusory, including Isaac Newton's picture of a universally ticking clock.

Similarly, Einstein himself described: "people like us, who believe in physics, know that the distinction between past, present and future is only a stubbornly persistent illusion".

As it is said until you witness something with your eyes, in your present reality, it is nothing but illusion. Whereas people today are relying on most percentage of information that is not reaching them through their present but through all the other tools that mainly work for fiction and not reality. And sometimes illusion works in worse ways than this. It can fool you even if you are witnessing with your own eyes, like the concept of mirage, which as per science is an optical illusion caused by various atmospheric factors, especially the appearance of water in a desert or on a hot road caused by the refraction of light from the sky by heated air, but in layman's language it's a lie. So, illusion and experiences that stems from it are so ingrained in all of us and our lives yet not given much credit to the impact it can have on each one of our lives.

In another description, mirage also means an unrealistic hope or wish that cannot be achieved, the way today an illusionary world projects such mindless aspirations on people and make them live in a constant hustle of achieving the same. Making them either dislike their present or not being grateful for wherever they are or whatever they have in their lives.

So, in the beginning we discover fifth dimension only through flashes, brief insights of people having intuitive flashes that have altered and changed the pattern of their entire life. Great inventions and music have come from the fifth dimension in a flash. Followed by years of working all the details through third and fourth dimensions. All this leading to awakened psychics entering the fifth dimensions and enabling them to read patterns of the future and passed through the third eye. Hence, if we put this to an example we can say, that great inventions which have no real explanations like music have come from the fifth dimension in a flash, followed by years of great work yes, but the still, small voice, or the inner voice, the intuition comes directly from the fifth dimension, and we experience its presence through these forms of art. The third eye functions from the 5th and 6th dimensions. Awakened psychics enter the fifth dimension and can read the patterns of the past which are going to design the future through the third eye and 6th sense only.

Sometimes when this illusion game goes wrong people call it delusion. Which is a very plain example of the saying 'if the end is good, everything is good', but if the result is messed up whole idea is rejected and fails. So, illusion is seen as delusion when it fails to manifest itself on the grounds of reality. It is believed that delusion is a desire lacking action. Whereas if action is playing an equal part with intention, it can turn into a manifestation.

'The future, though it remains unknown to you, seems to be written already'.

In the time dimension it is believed—past, present and future of everything can be different for all. The pace, the change, growth and evolution can vary for everything. There is nobody behind or ahead it is just the point where their journey is at, and it cannot be compared. There is no point of ego, one cannot be superior because one is ahead of another, because that may change in the blink of an eye. It is also called the wheel of time which keeps circling back to square one and changes everything that comes its way for good or bad. And it's also the reason why they say future is here, because the one who is living in the future is still living at the same time as one who is still living in past, both present together but breathing and functioning in different dimension at the same time. That is 5th dimension showing its presence amalgamating with 4th dimension.

The main cause of concern arises from this - what would you do if you enter in the 5th dimension whilst living amongst people who are still operating from the initial dimensions? Does this gap leave you no choice but to rule over them? Do we have differences like we have today based upon rich and poor, powerful and powerless due to this very distinction of the dimension in which one is leading their lives? How do we manage this distinction and survive amongst those who aren't even close to where you started? Or do you set yourself up yet for another battlefield with the mob psychology, because you do not think like them, and you stand out?

The Pursuit Of Consciousness

'Call it what you want yeah'
'Our generation's idea of karma'

Karma: The only way to serve God
("Work – the only thing you can count on, everything else is fragile")

Apart from the very ordinary meaning of "work" that we see today as something which is required for us to pay our bills and allows us to live in society with our chin up so that we don't have to live under anybody's shadow just because they pay for our food and shelter, work has all sorts of magnificent purposes attached to it. As Krishna in the holy scriptures of Geeta has mentioned that in order for mankind to be sure if they are serving god or not they should seek that longing through work, and here work does not denote any kind of work of status - work can be any work as long as it involves the person's devotion and intention of service. This work plays many important roles in the life of mankind who could travel far with this spirit in him. This energy is boundless and can progress as much as desired. When individuals have no meaningful work to channel this energy into, it can lead to stress and anxiety. Therefore, engaging in purposeful tasks helps individuals to transform stress into the energy necessary to complete their work. And that is the best utilisation of that energy, at least before one finds his sole purpose because if purpose is realised then this energy is automatically directed towards making that purpose come into reality effortlessly. And this work is the only way we can be sure that we are going closer to our dream world, doesn't matter at what pace and how long it takes, but it's better to keep crawling each second than to run fast for a short time just to be demotivated and stop later.

"Work as if you were a stranger in this land. Do not bind yourself in bondage to anything. That is terrible." – Vivekananda

The impact of karmas lies in the very existence of karmas that we unknowingly perform in our daily lives. It comprises of the thoughts we are feeding on and designing. Each action is based upon those thoughts. So, karmas are the accumulation of our thoughts in each second of our lives which then puts us in the choices we find ourselves in because of it. Karma lies in the very intention you possess about everything in your life.

It is quite straightforward to assess each of your intentions against your moral compass to determine whether you are accumulating positive or negative karma. If I choose to speak ill of others repeatedly, I am ultimately creating a detrimental environment for myself, not necessarily in terms of materials and resources, but rather in the quality of life that I am shaping around me. Judgement is the crucial part of it all in creating good or bad karma. Not being able to put oneself in the shoes of others and judging their choices all the time because your current life situation allows you to do so now doesn't guarantee that you will never end up at the receiving end or in a similar situation as other person whom you are judging today. That is basically lacking insight of life for anyone who judges one based on their current situation in life. As we say, nothing stays forever. Success or failure are just part of one's life, life which has higher meaning than these superficial subjective definitions of success and failure. Life is bigger than that; it is the amalgamation of everything that one can experience and possess in human form and there are no limits to it. We also know that the universe does not differentiate between dos and don'ts or light and darkness. Everything which runs using energy is valid, its existence is not a lie but a big truth beyond the capacity to be understood by any one of us, and life is a combination of all these truths revealing themselves in their own time. So, karma plays a crucial role in helping us unfold something so uncertain as life. And being ignorant of the importance of it only leads to error for which we then blame God. Realising the importance of karma sets human beings on this fundamental conviction that all of it eventually would function as it should in the best way possible utilising everything it has in its best form.

"Do not rely on the outer world as your measuring stick for your own spiritual growth. Rely on your response to the outer world to determine how much you have grown".

So, each karma is directly proportional to one's belief system. If I have the firm belief that the principles I abide by are enough to keep me going in my life the way I want, my karmas are justified. But if my intuition is making me doubt those principles in anyway whatsoever, I am required to reflect and see from where that doubt is coming. Self-doubt is sometimes the result of a lack of confidence yes, but intuition is supposed to be always right. It does not arise from any fear, envy, anger, hatred or lack of confidence. Unless your intuition is pure and not a product of your mind being intoxicated by outside forces like alcohol, weed, or internal ones like pride or doubt, it can be considered trustworthy. An effective belief system that remains free of doubts about your actions signifies quality in those actions, implying confidence in their correctness. Having conviction in the meaningfulness and importance of your actions, believing in your goals, and having confidence in achieving them is a sound beginning.

We see an example of this in Steve Job's "reality distortion field" which was a personal refusal to accept limitations, which were imposed by outside forces, which stood in the way of his ideas. He believed that any difficulty was surmountable. This 'field' of his was so strong that he was able to convince others that they too, could achieve the impossible, and that helped him in creating a team of people with a success mindset which helped him in achieving whatever he set out to achieve.

And this approach stays as long as you need if it is independent of any opposite thoughts and emotions that can weaken its existence. To begin with feeling no pressure whatsoever, just reboot and redo if you need to. And stop worrying about anything that is out of your control. Save up your energy wherever possible so that it can be utilised in the right place at the right time.

Now that we can see that with so much emphasis on the nature of our karmas, everything that happens to us in our lives naturally shifts the responsibility on ourselves. This means that there is no need to attribute responsibility to another party. It also eliminates the rationale for not addressing our own circumstances based on the assumption that external factors are solely responsible for outcomes.

As accountability returns to us, we face increased pressure regarding how to address actions from the past that may have been inappropriate. This can provoke concern about previous deeds—whether committed knowingly or unknowingly—and their potential consequences. That is where the religious scriptures help us. For example, the Bible which says,

Isaiah 43:25

"I am he who blots out your transgressions for my own sake, and I will not remember your sins. I---yes, I--- alone ----will blot out your sins for my own sake and will never think of them again".

Which clearly suggest that the higher power which we generally refer to as God or higher consciousness does not really think like we do. We as people who generally operate on lower frequencies, have a mind which ruminates on what has happened, good or bad. God does not like to ruminate on anything and loves to move on, but the condition is that you should love to move on to the next chapter as well. The moment of realisation should be the last time you spend your thought on something that no longer serves you and the moment you decide not to repeat that sin, believe that God has forgotten it too not just for one's own sake but for god's sake as well. So as soon as you shift the nature of your karmas, the direction of your destiny can also be changed like that. Just your heart and your mind should be in alignment with the needs of your body and soul and your mind should be willing to work in your interest rather than working against you.

Karma's significance is evident in how it relates to suffering: what truly matters is not the hardship itself, but our reaction to it. This concept is illustrated by two arrows. The first arrow represents what we experience from the world—positive or negative—which we cannot control, as it stems from others' actions. This initial suffering is inevitable since we interact with and depend on society and nature.

The second arrow refers to our reaction to initial pain. It is not just our actions that cause pain, but also how we respond to it and to others. Enlightenment seeks to address this second arrow by encouraging us to respond thoughtfully rather than react impulsively. This approach helps shape a positive environment both within us and for our loved ones, breaking negative cycles. The key is to understand the difference between 'responding' and 'reacting', aiming only to respond to uncontrollable external forces.

The concept of the second arrow suggests that one's identity is shaped by what one loves, rather than what loves them. This implies that an individual's current state is influenced by their mindset. When a person becomes emotionally affected by the initial negative experience (the first arrow), it can lead to further distress. However, the decision to react to this initial experience (the second arrow) is within the individual's control. Thus, the lasting negative impact is often due to the nature of the second arrow rather than the first one.

As they say,

"I make whatever I feel like, so when I am feeling terrible, I am making the candy terrible".

Recognizing the significance of karma, the doer often contemplates what personal benefit may be derived from their actions. However, the essence of karma lies in selfless dedication to one's work, without concern for the potential outcomes. The underlying principle is that the results of every effort and hard work should be devoted to a higher power. Any fruits or achievements should be entirely dedicated to the divine. This approach emphasizes the importance of detaching oneself from both the work and its results. The quality of being rationally detached from anything that has been taken on in one's life is given utmost important. Even if one is expected to live to work, work does not come above the powers of one's soul. So, to protect one's soul from the first arrow, rational detachment is expected by the doer towards the duties they perform. It also helps one to protect oneself from all the disappointments and dissatisfactions one may develop with respect to the result they get. So now every result, no matter if they come out be tasteful or tasteless are dedicated to God. By following this the doer tends to protect one's soul from the result and doesn't get demotivated when something does not turn out to be as planned or expected, as now the sole purpose behind performing that duty is just the dedication of it all to one supreme power which is God. So, work done is work dedicated.

But sometimes this gets tough for people to digest because people who come from lower dimensions and who operate on lower frequencies in life think money is the goal. And having to achieve wisdom means just utilising that wisdom to fulfil one's never-ending desires. But this is a thought which has nothing to do with one's life purpose or the ultimate truth. In effect it is a hoax designed by the world or illusionary perceptions to trap people and waste their energy on things that only matter on a superficial level, and not in deep reality.

Eureka: The Elixir Within
(Meditation is the formula to defy the rule of gravity)

The whole idea is to reach a point of beyond suffering… that is the whole bone of contention.

Life is, if seen in any way as controversial is because of the way we need to deal with all sorts of sufferings coming our way in every aspect of our life. Major journeys talk about the need for having strength in our being so that we can go through life safe and unaffected by the heaps of obstacles coming our way. So, all the brainstorming circles back to what is that one solution that we need as humanity to ensure for ourselves a life of constant mental and emotional peace which then would help us in shaping our physical life on the same lines. It is that one last attempt to make our lives worth living, each second, we breathe, to breathe strength in to our mind and body and a sense of comfort in our soul. And my search was to find an elixir like that, a billion-dollar solution, which unites the whole world and ends up completing the picture, in search of that lost puzzle.

And I found my answer. A traditional answer. A lot of you have already understood it to be meditation yes, but what is meditation? Even that is different for each one of us, the recipe may differ yes, but the process is the same. A meditation like that which can fit all. As weird as it sounds for those who are not ready to receive it yet, my duty is not to exclude anyone. My role is to put it out, because if it worked for me why should I not help others who are at least seeking it or need it?

"Naam-Jaap"

Let us start from scratch. Let us begin from naam Jaap. What is naam Jaap? It basically means repeating (jaap) or remembering a name or mantra (or Mantram). It can be any mantra or name of your choice. One can take one's favourite deity's name to start naam Jaap. It can be any trusted name of your choice that your subconscious mind can recite whenever left alone, on its own, a deity whose general characteristics you would want to imbibe and inculcate in your being, Like some people rely on "Hari", "Raam", "Radhe", "Krishna", "Radha swami", "Sadh guru", "Jesus" or "Allah". It can be any name of your choice.

Says Swami Satchidananda-

"You can perform Japa, the repetition of a mantra or sacred word, during your day-to-day work. Then, when it becomes a habit, even when you are working intensely a portion of the mind will keep repeating the mantras always. That means you have locked one end of your chain to a holy place, while the rest of the chain remains still in the outside world".

If you have never practiced mantra meditation before, the process of reciting a mantra may appear rather mechanical. But the repetition of mantra/name is anything but robotic. With regular practice, you will find that Japa practice will lead you to a much deeper understanding of yourself as you encounter new layers of your mind. Wants and needs. desires and hopes, duties and obligations, ideals and aspirations surface in your awareness. From meditation to meditation, life unfolds under your inner gaze, asking you to witness it in its entirety. A mantra serves as a kind of centring device during this process. It offers a resting place for the everyday mind. It collects distracting energies. It brings spiritual insights forward, so that you can integrate them into daily life. Just as great music transforms a listener, a mantra gradually lifts and transforms your mind.

As much as it sounds traditional and religious, as this concept is popularised by Sanatan Dharma where names like 'Radhe', 'Hari', 'Ram' are chosen for Naam Japa, if you understand the science behind chanting mantra, you will realise in fact that all the religions talk about taking god's name incessantly. Yes, its science and logic is not explained to us thoroughly but if we dig deeper, one would realise that you are not asked to take god's name to glorify that god, but you are supposed to take god's name so that your ever wandering mind can find a stable place to rest whenever it is left on its own instead of wandering to places which would not help one in any way.. A super active mind as the one we all have, needed its haven. Where it can rest in the times when there is no need for constructive thought. And that resting place is this naam-Japa which basically replaces the 'overthinking' state of mind.

What makes us so sure that it works? Well, in the yoga tradition, a key element of meditation is the repetition of a sound or a prayer- a mantra – which focuses the mind and becomes a source of inner balance and well-being.

The process of mentally repeating a mantra is called Japa, which literally means "muttering" in Sanskrit. With practice when you are repeating the name on repeat mode within yourself, Japa becomes well rooted in the mind, and the sound of the mantra flows continuously from moment to moment. It may flow slowly or at a moderate pace. After considerable practice, the mantra may pulse very rapidly. In this case. meditation with the mantra flows without exertion. This phase of practice is called Ajapa Japa, or effortless repetition.

Adepts sometimes refer to this phase of meditation as "listening to the mantra" the mantra becomes audible without mental exertion. And the inner space of the mind is filled with its sound. The resulting practice is effortless and delightful, but it occurs only after considerable experience with a mantra.

"It's an attempt at elimination of thought patterns that keep you stuck".

Thus, naam Japa gives you ultimate happiness and bliss. The tale of Samudra Manthana from Hindu mythology narrates the churning of the ocean of milk by gods and demons to obtain the nectar of immortality. Naam Japa is a similar churning of your mind which gives inner peace and happiness filling you with a sense of immortality. Your soul becomes shielded and nothing from the surrounding can touch your aura or affect the core of it in anyway.

Also basically, you can mind your own business in the true sense when you dwell on that name of your choice. How one chooses the name depends upon what qualities they want to imbibe in oneself, what thoughts come into your head about the name you have been repeating. It is experienced that you are naturally going to imbibe those qualities in you, that you associate with that name in your head, when you are constantly meditating on that name, and your entire body, each cell in your body is aligned to the rest of the body, mind and soul at that very moment. And your entire body can be in synchronicity with the other. What a perfect moment for a body to start healing than when your entire body is in synchronicity with the mind of the one whose name you are chanting. And imagine if you can do that anytime and any moment. It does not matter if you are in the middle of a very important task, you can still meditate and keep your body, mind and soul safe from outside forces of any sort.

"Elixir of Ajapa-japa, cannot be destroyed by any illusion if it's caught by you once".

So, what happens when it finally starts working? That is an experience you can go through only once you decide to reach that point, once you start walking that path. Practitioners describe it as a deep sense of peace and subtle waves of calm flowing through one's body and mind when you repeat that god's name. It can be seen as a real psychological, neurological and spiritual phenomenon, not just something imagined. We can really feel the changes happening through both the rational and spiritual lens:

Repeating a mantra quietens down the brain. It slows down mental chatter and takes you on a ride to peaceful journey at least in one's head. This rhythm reduces activity in the default mode network (DMN)—the part of your brain involved in overthinking, ego, and worry.

That wave of peace which you feel when you are by default chanting a name is followed by waves of calm going through your entire body which in turn calms you down as if you are on some therapy constantly. This is the best feeling of it all. It is like you are giving your body, mind and soul some treatment. It feels like you are doing some kind of favour on your soul. From a scientific point of view, it appears that your body is shifting into a relaxed, parasympathetic state (rest and digest mode). It is the opposite of stress mode (fight or flight mode).

Repetition, especially when linked to emotion or reverence (like saying god's name) can also trigger release of serotonin(well-being), oxytocin (connection, warmth) and dopamine (reward, focus).

Reaching a meditative state like that is also associated with deep meditation, relaxation, and spiritual flow. And since they are often active during prayer, chanting, or mindful breathwork, Naam Jaap appears to be the easiest, least demanding and free of cost therapy which we can avail of at any moment of our lives.

If we see from a spiritual angle, the repetitive chanting of your choice of a divine name also becomes an anchor, a point of return—a sacred, simple focus that pulls your awareness out of chaos and into the present. Also, faith and surrender like that can easily help quieten the ego which we are all knowingly or unknowingly holding on to. When you recite with emotion, there is often a surrender of control. That humility and connection can dissolve anxiety and soften your sense of separateness. In other words, it will naturally inculcate rational detachment in your heart and soul which is one of the most difficult principles to adopt in the world full of interdependence and interconnectedness.

And not to forget how this act which is peaceful when done on repeat can open a resonance channel for you. Whether you see it as God, the divine field or simply inner truth.

The process of chanting a name has its own stages which takes you on this journey of self-purging. Not just spiritually and psychologically but it also cleanses your aura from inside and out.

Emotionally: it comes in pulses, not all at once. That is how the nervous system starts to release tensions. When you see it in action, many describe it like vibrations or ripples. As if something subtle is moving inside of them. And not to forget spiritually, its often-called Shanti (peace) or Ananda (bliss) in yogic or devotional traditions-- not forced but arising gently.

Although we already understand how everything in our lives appears to be woven like a web, interconnected and tightly knit, treating one thread of the web can automatically help us solve the others. Which takes us to the physical effects of chanting a name, the changes that you would start noticing in time with your own eyes are immeasurable., If one continues reciting god's name – whether as mantra, prayer, or mindful repetition- it can bring very real, measurable physical changes in one's body, brain and overall health over time. It is like a reset to your system, everything that was done to your body emotionally, spiritually and physically and is innate in your system now without even your choice, chanting a name can help dissolve all those effects into nothingness and would set your body on a default mode to start your journey afresh. And this time with your consciousness playing the lead role. These effects have been supported by both modern neuroscience and ancient spiritual traditions.

Hence the physical changes can be seen by regular repetition of a calming word, or phrase. How it rewires your brain to become more resilient to stress. Over time your default reaction shifts from anxiety to calmness. Since name chanting and meditation helps in nervous system rewiring.it can also help your mind to build its neuroplasticity. Brain scans show reduced activity in the amygdala (fear centre) and increased activity in the prefrontal cortex (decision making, empathy and calmness).

Hence one becomes less reactive, more emotionally stable and mentally clearer.

Chanting also slows down your breathing, which directly slows your heart rate. Your body with regular practice starts to activate the parasympathetic nervous system—bringing rest, repair, and balance.

Meditation, like repetition, is also linked to the upregulation of beneficial genes, including those related to immunity and longevity. It also downregulates genes related to inflammation and aging. Therefore, stronger immune system, slower aging process and better overall vitality. A lot can be promised when you choose to take this elixir.

There are millions of more favourable changes to witness as you go ahead with naam Jaap in life. And these changes can be subjective to everyone for the level of faith and devotion they have in it, how much they trust it with their whole body. It is a long journey which each human being should be able to experience and come out on the other side, with their box of blessings unlocked exclusive to them and that can be shared with the rest of us. Experiencing greater joy in everyday moments and developing a heightened sense of intuition can enhance one's ability to attune to inner guidance and instincts. Your presence becomes compassionate for others to be around you. And eventually you develop a deeper silence in your soul not because you stop chanting the name but because the name and you are no longer separate.

Out of all the advantages we could see, and we are yet to discover the profoundly significant effect of chanting a holy name on repeat at the back of your mind, is its ability to let you perform your duties, fulfilling your responsibilities towards the world while the name keeps working its magic. So basically, we can witness a sign of integration in this type of devotion—a merging of Karma yoga and Bhakti Yoga---the path of action, and the path of love.

Most people think they must withdraw from the world to go inward but this experience is something rare: god's name does not pull you away from life, it pours into it.

Hence chanting does not interrupt your work, it is infusing it with more benefits. Here you are not splitting your day between 'worldly tasks' and 'spiritual time', in fact you are working through devotion, living inside remembrance and turning each action into an offering, not by ritual but by presence.

This is the essence of karma done in bhakti:

It is what the Gita hints at when Krishna says, "offer every action to me".

The best part about this whole experience is, chanting a name or "naam Jaap' as we call it, does not detach us from the world. In fact, it creates a deeper intimacy with it. Because chanting god's name like this is not taking you away from responsibility rather it is making you more available, more loving, more grounded. Which means, you are not escaping the world, but you are sanctifying it. As you are not distracted by the divine, but you are accompanied by it. This is what saints called "Smaran within karma" ----remembrance inside action. Neurologically chanting sacred names slows the breath, stabilises the nervous system, and activates the vagus nerve leading to calm alertness, restoration of energy and physical and emotional healing over time.

The whole experience does not require analysis. It just flows, and flows and flows.

www.ingramcontent.com/pod-product-compliance
Lightning Source LLC
Chambersburg PA
CBHW052119070526
44584CB00017B/2557